Beauty for ASHES

The Story Behind the Breakthrough

Published by: C Lenoir Publishing, LLC
www.CLenoirPublishing.com
@CLenoirPublishing

C Lenoir Publishing, LLC books may be purchased for educational, business, or sales promotional use. For more information, permission requests, and wholesale inquiries, please contact C Lenoir Publishing, LLC, at read@clenoirpublishing.com. Thank you for your support of the author's rights.

First Edition: March 2022
Book Designer: Mandi Lynn
Front Cover Photograph – Kevin Malone | MDK Productions and Photography
Interior Book Illustrations – Shakielah Frorup | Z~n~Z Custom Designz
Back Cover Photograph – Jamel Overstreet | Overstreet Media Services

Unless otherwise noted, Scriptures are taken from the Zondervan NIV study Bible. (2002). Barker, K. (Ed.). Rev. ed. Grand Rapids, MI: Zondervan.

Tyndale House Publishers. (2004). Holy Bible: New Living Translation. Wheaton, Ill: Tyndale House Publishers.

King James Bible. (2008). Oxford University Press. (Original work published 1769)

ISBN- 978-1-7374838-7-8

BEAUTY FOR ASHES

The Story Behind the Breakthrough

By

Nicole E. Holmes

This book is dedicated to the people who have suffered in silence long enough. It's your time now. Your breakthrough is waiting on you. Let's go, we've got work to do.

TABLE OF CONTENTS

FOREWORD

In every church there are pew members who find comfort in sitting in the same seat, on the same row, Sunday after Sunday. Well, on the third row, in the first seat at St. James Baptist Church in Baconton, Ga., there was Nicole, Sunday after Sunday. Even though Nicole participated in the worship experience, she was still bound on the inside. The altar became a place of rest and reassurance for her, but she needed so much more.

At first, I really didn't know that much about my loving dear friend, but I knew that there was a struggle going on. So, I reached out to her, as God led me, and I took her under my wing. I could see that she had the concealed passion of a dancer, a worshipper. She was not aware of the anointing on her life. I thank God for using me to bless her life and my very own life as well. It's a sweet blessing just to know her.

God kept saying, "I'll use her if she'll only open up and

allow herself to be used." Little did she know that she was in the right position for purpose, the right position to receive her deliverance, and most of all, she was in the right position for God to get the glory out of her life!!!

So, I began to invite her to the Dance Ministry. I kept telling her that she was a dancer and that we would wait for her. She kept saying, "Who me?" And I kept saying, "Yes, you Love."

When she gave God a yes, He began to dance with her and He revealed the true Worshipper/Warrior within (a reference to John 4:23). And my, my, my, I can now go through my archive of videos of Minister Nicole Holmes ministering, offering hope and healing to others. Yes, I said Minister Nicole Holmes. She's no longer on the third row, in the first seat, but she's on the front line for the Lord. She is a very powerful vessel for the Kingdom and she's a breathtaking instrument of praise. I encourage you to read and share Nicole's amazing testimony of how she went from Bitter to Better, and how dance saved her life. To God be the Glory!!!

Minister Carolyn Price
Grateful Praise Dance Ministry Leader
St. James Missionary Baptist Church
Baconton, Ga.

ACKNOWLEDGEMENTS

First, I want to thank God for taking me through this journey. I'm grateful He chose me, I'm grateful He called me out, I'm grateful He equipped me, and I'm grateful He set me free. It was not easy, but it was definitely necessary. I also want to thank my mom, Leona, and my dad, Rubio, for always being there for me no matter what. Thanks to all my siblings, my family, and friends who stayed the path with me, never letting me give up. A special thank you to Mrs. (Minister) Carolyn Price and Mrs. (Minister) Bratisha Covin for always holding me accountable and pushing me to keep writing. It has been quite a long journey. Thanks again to everyone for the encouragement and prayers. Blessings to you all.

INTRODUCTION

How in the world did I come to write a book? I knew I had a lot to say, I experienced a lot, and I had to release it somehow. Several years ago, I wrote my very first article for my church's newsletter at St. James Baptist Church. A few days after that, my pastor called me and said, "Nicole Holmes, you got a book in you." I didn't pay him any attention. I brushed it off and went on like he didn't say anything. Although I dismissed what he said at the time, I would still find myself writing in my journal. I had already started writing and didn't even realize it. I've been writing in my journal since 2015 and now, six years later, I'm finally writing this book. As I reread my journal, all I saw was the residue of memories of a life filled with pain. Pain and hurt bled from those pages. I've been through a lot, experienced a lot, learned a lot, and most of all, I've survived a lot. I knew I wasn't alone in this, though.

My spirit said, "Do something with it." I was being pulled

towards broken women and people who were hurting just like me. That pull would not leave me. I knew I had to do something. I knew at least one person needed my story. Someone needed to know just like I know now that I wasn't the only one feeling like this. It was finally clear to me that the old cliché "There's purpose in your pain" was in fact true. My story, my testimony, my pain have now become someone else's lifeline. I had no idea how I would get it done, but what I did know was I could no longer be silent. I had been smothered long enough. So, I put pen to paper and poured it out. This meant that I would have to be transparent, vulnerable, and ready to share my history even if it offended a few people. As raw as it was, it would hopefully save someone's future. I pray it does just that, and that this book gives you clarity, a peace of mind, and most of all, freedom from every area that has you bound to pain. "You sure about this, God?" OK, here it goes.

WHERE IT ALL BEGAN

I am not the person I used to be those many years ago. Let me take you back to the days when I was lost and didn't even know I needed to be found. In 1993, I came to the state of Georgia by way of the U.S. Virgin Islands. Born and raised there, I left home at the age of 17 to attend college at Albany State College (now known as Albany State University). This was a difficult transition as I did not have any family there and I didn't know anyone. I quickly had to adjust to a new culture, and worse, the constantly changing weather (which by the way, I'm still not used to). Going home was out of the question. I wanted to be grown and to be on my own, so I had to stick it out. You know how we get when we leave home.

As time went on, I made a few friends, and being on my own and adjusting to my new life became a little easier to cope with. I was doing well, and school wasn't so bad. I was partying, having a good time doing whatever I wanted whenever I wanted. Why? Because I was "grown." One day in the school cafeteria, I noticed a football player staring at me (let him tell it, I was the one staring at him). My friend Kristy knew him and introduced us. His name was Kevin. Shortly after that, we started dating and eventually became a couple. About a year or so later, I got pregnant and had my first child at the age of 21. A huge disappointment to my parents, but what happened had already happened.

Life for me as I knew it was over. I now had to focus on bringing a child into this world. I had no clue what I was doing; all I knew was it had to be done. I had to grow up fast and nothing since then has ever been about me. There was no more hanging out and partying. I now had to find a job and go to work. School took a backseat; it took me almost six years to graduate from college, but I did. Failure was not an option, but my oh my, the struggle was real. I wasn't alone in this. I had help from my parents, my siblings, my friends at school, and, most of all, my child's father (who later became my husband).

Although I had resources, for some reason I still felt alone. It wasn't until later on I realized I suffered from postpartum depression. Yeah, it's a real thing and I had it bad. But because I didn't know what it was and why I was feeling the way I was feeling, it turned into something else. Now according to medical science, postpartum normally lasts for six to eigh weeks. Well, for me it never ended. As I said, it turned into something else. But because I couldn't figure it out, anger and frustration settled in me like it paid rent to live there.

Now, I wasn't angry at my child at all, in fact, I loved her very much. What happened was I was angry with myself. It was all internal; I felt as though I had stolen my own young adult days from myself. I missed it all. That anger and frustration bled into everything I did and said. But it had become normal. It was now a part of my everyday life. And at this point, I didn't want to change because it was all I knew. I had become comfortable, and somehow it made me feel stronger and invincible in some way. How crazy is that? Well keep reading, it gets worse.

As time went on, I had my second child and eventually got married. You'd think that would've changed things, but it didn't. The only thing that changed was my last name. What remained were the emotions I hoarded. The anger and frustration split off into several different branches. As we all know, whatever you feed the most is what will grow. So imagine what I was producing with anger as the water and seed. All I can say now is "WOW." But the truth is the truth. Those branches of bitterness, isolation, hate, being quick-tempered, pain, hurt, and so much more had now consumed me. The problem with this was I still didn't now what it was. Like I said, it had become normal. So buried the root and covered the branches as if all was well. I had become very good at appearing to have it all together. Here's the problem with that: I had become so good at "pretending" that I had even convinced myself that I was cured and that all really was well. I thought I was happy and had single-handedly fixed everything. But what I created was a volcano waiting to erupt.

WHO HAD I BECOME?

Years went by and life still seemed normal. Or so I thought. I was still me, but now I had no reflection. Stick with me, it'll make sense in a minute. Have you ever looked at yourself in the mirror and saw nothing? You see your reflection of course, but have you ever seen nothing? I did a mirror check one day and just stared at myself for what seemed like an eternity. I had no answers, I had no clue. I knew my name but that was it. I don't know this person I see before me. Who are you, and where did you come from? I could hear my inner self saying, "You're lost, you're angry, you're hurting, you need help." It wasn't until later on that I realized it was the Holy Spirit talking to me, trying to intercede on my behalf, but we'll touch on that later. But hearing all those things in my head infuriated me. I felt crazy and out of control, and I did not like that at all. I needed to be in control. That was my survival tactic.

So, what did I do? I'll tell you what I did. I created a whole new identity led by a monster called pride. I became all I needed. I drowned out the rational voices in my head and replaced them with everything opposite of what I had heard. So now there are two of me to handle. Like one wasn't enough. So now I'm in fight mode, because of course there can only be one winner. This battle was an everyday fight. Can you imagine fighting against yourself daily? Who really wins? The stronger version of myself was winning, but at what cost? I was slowly killing myself and didn't even know it. How many of us are guilty of that even to this day? We think we're winning, but in reality, we're actually losing. I mean really, how can you win against yourself if you're fighting to keep a delusion alive? But at the time, I didn't see it like that. I saw it as me protecting myself from the world. Protecting myself against the pain caused by others. Protecting myself against all vulnerabilities. I had become a bunker. As we all know, a bunker is a reinforced shelter typically for use in wartime. Well, I was at war, and nobody was getting in.

This way of thinking caused a lot of distance from the people I actually needed in my life. But because I was always a war, I saw everyone as the enemy. No one could be trusted, no even for a second. Yeah, it was that serious. Now don't get m wrong, I had people in my life. I just didn't let them in. I had m kids, my husband, and a few friends. They were all restricted t the surface, though. Intimacy was out of the question, and the only got to see what I wanted them to see. By this time, the kids got older, and I eventually got divorced. That was the straw that broke the camel's back. I became angrier and now bitter. A bad combination to have. That was a huge blow to my ego, and I had lost control of that situation. And as I've said before, I needed to be in control. My husband used to say, "You're so mean and evil," and it used to make my blood boil. But looking back now, was he even wrong? That was his experience and how he felt even if I denied or dismissed it. That was a hard pill to swallow. But I didn't swallow it just yet; I used it as fuel to keep me going. Little did I know, it was burning me alive.

The pain I was feeling and experiencing, that I thought was coming from other people, was really the pain I had inflicted on myself. The need to protect myself from said pain would be the reason it got to me in the first place. "How could this happen? I don't deserve this." I kept asking and saying all these things and more to myself. I'm not only mad with everybody, now I'm mad with God. "How could You let these things happen to me? Do You not see what is being done to me?" His response to me was, "The weight of your heart is because you personalize everything, you think everything and everyone is against you. It's not always personal, but it's preparation for a deeper understanding as to why you're really here...Your heart has been divided into multiple pieces and you've been broken since 1998." What a revelation that was. I had been

13

patching the pieces together all the while covering who I really was at the time and fighting against who I was to become. I was pretending to be something I wasn't. Imagine all that time, I was someone else and didn't even realize it. This was why I was lost and had no clue who I had become. I had to go back and find myself. But the problem was, it had been so long that I didn't even remember where I left ME at.

Reality was setting in and this time I couldn't deny it. It was burning a hole in my soul. The damage had spread all over and consumed all of me. It damaged the real me. The me I was hiding. The me I thought I was protecting. But it wasn't protection at all, in fact, it was murder. God wanted me to see it. He wanted me to feel every bit of it. To get through this I needed to go back to that mirror and acknowledge my reflection. But not just in my head, I would have to speak what I saw out loud. A memory and/or conviction hits differently when you hear it audibly from your own mouth. But why, God? Why this way? You know we always have to ask God why. But His response was what I needed to be reminded of. He was showing me the fight was already won. I had convinced myself that the loss made me unworthy of His win for me, I kept creating a new opponent. Catch this now, it wasn't another person, it was another version of myself. One who I thought was even stronger than the last one. One who was attached to the root. One of the many branches that had formed. That is who I recruited each

14

time. I was giving life to things God had already said He would burn away if only I would release them. I'd become so tunnel-visioned that I couldn't even see His hand stretched out to me. I couldn't help but wonder, why would my mind have me going to bed with no sleep, looking at an empty spot; why I kept to myself most of the time; why I stared at the walls and it bled my tears; why the only echo I heard in my home was that of a dying heart?

It got louder, harder, and more painful as the days went by. I couldn't figure it out, I just kept wondering and asking. You know how we get sometimes. We play the victim's role (woe is me). But He made it very clear that I was feeling this way only because I didn't believe He would do just what His word said or that He had something better for me. I couldn't receive any of it because I wouldn't let go of what I was holding onto. But the truth is, I didn't know how to at the time. So I kept what was familiar, as it posed no threat to me. I had become desensitized to reality. This dysfunction had become attached to everything. My job, my relationship with my children, my friends (what was left of them), and most of all, my purpose and destiny. God made me realize that nothing would change until I first believed. I was reminded of a lot of things, one being that I was living in a 360-degree atmosphere; I always came back to where I started from and repeated the same cycles over and over again. But God offered me a 180-degree atmosphere on one condition: I stop fighting, come out of the ring, and let Him take over. That sounded good. I wanted to be free, but being free would mean giving up control. God didn't give up on me, though. He knew I couldn't break away on my own. He said, "Get out of the ring, take off the gloves, face Me, seek my face, yield to my will, and let Me lead." And then silence overcame me. A type of silence I've never experienced before. That silence was deafening. And in that silence I heard, "You are where you're supposed to be." The lesson is there and so are the answers. But I would never see what He sees or know what He knows about me until I believed it. The sad part about this is I believed it all, just not for myself. How could I believe it for others and not for myself? Because if that were the case, that would make God a liar, which contradicts His word in Numbers 23:19 (NLT), "God is not a man, so He does not lie. He is not human, so He does not change His mind. Has He ever spoken and failed to act? Has He ever promised and not carried it through?" I wrestled back and forth with this verse. Finally He said (I think He was fed-up at this point), "You can take your last breath in a 360 or fulfilled in a 180." Nothing else was said. Decisions, decisions, decisions. So many times we take what seems to be the easy path in order to avoid having to give up certain things and/or to do something different. And that just what I did. I chose the 360 paths. I chose to remain where was and would always return to.

ANGRY AND BITTER

When you travel a path that's comfortable it never leaves room for growth. My only option — or what I thought was my only option at the time — was to cultivate and harvest what was already inside me. And as you all know, whatever is inside you will come out, and whatever you feed will grow. I started to produce bad fruits of darkness. The one that took the lead was the fruit of bitterness. I resented everything and everyone. I was always on the defensive. So, to protect myself from further attacks, I put up a surrounding wall as strong as a military bunker. Nothing was getting in. I isolated myself from the world. Everything suffered, and somehow, I had become the bad guy in everyone's story. Well, at least that's what I told myself. OK, so that's what we're doing, let's play. Tit for tat mode activated. So now, in my mind, if you wanted to hate me, I could hate you even more. If you wanted to fight, we could fight. I was up for anything destructive.

As the young people would say, I was always on 100. I was ready to fire off at any and everybody. I had normalized this behavior because this was the only way I knew how to protect myself. I couldn't let them win. I wasn't about to lose again. No way, it wasn't happening. And that bitterness gave birth to a different kind of anger I couldn't control. This emotion was oftentimes misdirected at people, whom I later had to apologize to — including my children.

Studies show that there are three types of anger, which help shape how we react in certain situations. They are passive aggression, open aggression, and assertive aggression. Passive aggression is basically being silent. Where you have nothing to say and/or pretend nothing's wrong. Open aggression is where you lash out or become verbally or physically aggressive. This comes from a need to be in control (imagine that). Assertive aggression is much calmer. You're open to listen and talk things out rather than fight or argue. Well for me, assertive aggression was for weak people. I preferred passive aggression, then straight into open aggression. I wanted to project fear onto people versus being fearful. And I lived this way for years. So, you can imagine how hard it was for me to change. But at that point, I didn't even want to. I liked it. I had become a fighter and fighters never give up, they never quit, they WIN. So, the fight continued, and continued and continued.

Then one day, (all it takes is a moment sometimes) I became

so angry, my whole body began to tingle. A numbing, tingling feeling had consumed me. All I could see were burning red flames and I exploded. The volcano had finally erupted. I destroyed half of my apartment and had cuts all over my arms from broken glass. It took a long time for me to calm down and breathe normally. Have you ever felt that way? Like you literally can't breathe? It was an experience I will never forget. It wasn't until days later while cleaning up the mess that I came to the realization I was no longer in control. I was in fact out of control. That was a hard conviction to accept. People have said, "Whatever you try to control already controls you." I definitely believe that now. So, I had to ask God to show me a better way. I asked Him to point out what the real issues were. I needed to know where this anger and bitterness came from. I learned after the fact that my anger was a secondary emotion. It took away the focus on what the real problem was. It was my coping mechanism. That way of thinking almost cost me my life. Just like anything, to be angry is a choice, and it takes a lot of energy to stay that way. It will happen. We will get angry, but we just need to be clear on why we're angry in the first place. We have got to find the root cause and address it, that's the only way to release it and move on from it in peace. It's hard work, but it's definitely worth it in the end. The question is, are you ready to face it? Are you ready to not be angry? Are you ready to ask the hard questions and hear the true responses? Say it with me, YES, I AM!

ROOT PROBLEMS

How did I get here? Oh yeah, I chose familiarity. You'd think with what God said to me in Chapter 2 I'd be all better and you'd be done reading this book. Yet here we are. Now I'm wandering in the wilderness. Have you ever been in the wilderness? Wheeeeeew…. No map, no compass, no self-direction, no light, no nothing. As you can imagine, things only got worse for me. I took up that torch of pain and used it to make my way through everything. What I didn't realize was I was creating more branches. The branches spread to depression, anxiety, bondage, strongholds, etc. I'm hosting all these emotions inside me, and I inadvertently became their mother. And what does a good mother do? That's right, we nurture. I kept them alive, I helped them grow and I even protected them. Imagine that. It sounds crazy as I write it. I just couldn't let go. I had convinced myself that if I let go, I would lose and whatever I was fighting against would win.

And I don't like to lose.

But let's think about this for a moment. When people hurt us, intentionally or not, we often tend to hold onto it. How do we hold onto it? I'm glad you asked. We hold onto it by constantly replaying it in our minds. We hold onto it when we go out and tell everybody what so-and-so did to us. When we keep doing that, we never really address it and it becomes a part of us. The pain is fresh, like a layer of skin that never heals. It's in us. It's in our minds, our heartbeat, our thoughts, every breath we take in, and it's even in our soul. I've now become the weapon formed against myself. Yes, you read that right. Imagine that.

Let's be honest and ask ourselves the hard questions. Are you your number one enemy? Are you really the one against yourself? Are you the leader of the legion inside of you? For me, the answer was yes. Now I'm sure you remember the story in the Bible (in Mark 5) when Jesus meets a demon-possessed man and asked him for his name and his response was, "My name is Legion for we are many." Well, that's what I'm talking about. So my question is, are you the leader of the legion against yourself? Leading an army that consists of Bitterness, Anger, Loneliness, Hatred, Depression (that's a big one rarely talked about), Unforgiveness, Suicidal Thoughts, Mistrust, Dysfunction, Jealousy, Envy, and so on. These are just some that are part of the army, this legion, which we created, allowed in fed, nurtured, and held onto. All these things are toxic and will interfere with everything you try to do. So now that we have all these emotions and battles within ourselves, we've opened the door and are vulnerable to attacks from the enemy.

The enemy was having a field day in my life and was not letting up. But rather than ask for help, what do we do? We deny the truth so we don't have to deal with any of it or seem weak in front of others. Now just because you denied it doesn't mean it goes away. In fact, to keep it hidden you have to cover it with something else. For me, that covering came in the form of alcohol, food, sleeping, and isolation. How do you cover yours? What is your pacifier? Anything to get through the day, right? Right! So now I have that one, main issue: the original problem that was buried has now formed a root. That root was fed and spread into other issues that formed branches. Now I have a whole tree bearing fruits of dysfunction and it's killing me slowly. The same tree I eat and drink from every day. Now I'm asking myself, what is going on? Where did all this come from? Why am I being attacked from what seems like every direction? Well, it was the root problem that was ignored, denied, and buried that was the problem. It came back on me with vengeance. Have you ever experienced that? Yeah, I know exactly how that feels. It's a weight like no other. And I'm not talking about physical weight. I'm talking about mental weight. It's heavier than any object. Those of you who have been there before know exactly what I mean. All the mental weight turns to stress. Now my body is being attacked. It's like a cancer virus spreading all over, killing everything it touches.

Now my body hurts. I can't sleep, I can't eat, I can't even function. It's a mess. I'm now living and operating in dysfunction. But this type of living is dangerous for anyone. You risk the chance of becoming completely out of touch with reality. Now I'm at war again. But this time, it's too much. It's too heavy. Now I need to get rid of it. But how do I get rid of it while simultaneously holding onto it? How crazy is that? How can we let go of something we're holding onto? I'll give you a minute to let that sink in.

So now that we somewhat get it, what's next? Well, this is what I had to do. I had to ask for and acknowledge that I needed help. But from where? I'm in the wilderness and God has left me (well that's what I told myself). So, I step up, of course. "You got this, girl, you can do this on your own," is what I kept telling myself. I tried everything I could think of Nothing worked. I was weary and was ready to give up.

Then a still voice said, "Let go." Now, remember, I've been in this position for years and had not heard from God at all. So imagine how I felt when I did. Although I was relieved to hear those words, was I really ready for the follow-up action? Because in order to accept His help I would have to face the fear of the unknown, and I would no longer be in control. I kept asking myself, "Are you really ready this time?" First, let's break down what it means to let go. To let go means to relinquish one's grip on someone or something. It also means you get to find out who you really are and what you're really made of. You'll catch that later. Letting go will require you to face the facts, it holds you accountable (yes, you had a part in it), and it gives you a different perspective. Is it making sense to you? It did to me.

This reminds me of a time I went through a bad breakup (well for me it was bad). I invested my time with this person, I was all the way in it. I was head over heels, just nose wide open. A few months later it ended just as quickly as it started. I was crushed. I couldn't eat or sleep, and half the time I didn't go to work. I couldn't do and didn't want to do anything. Then one day, I came home and just lost it. I broke all the way down. The plan was to have a few shots (which I did), take a shower, get in bed, and turn off all access to the world. I got in the shower (I think I had more tears than the water coming out of the faucet). I cried out to God, "Make it stop," but the pain got heavier and heavier. I mean literally heavy. I could no longer stand up. I found myself crouched down at the bottom of my tub and God would not let me up. All I kept saying was, "Make it stop." I was in that position for a long time, and it wasn't until I stopped saying, "Make it stop," and said, "God, I yield," "I surrender to You, help me," — I'll never forget it — it was at that moment He physically let me up. I got out of the shower and got in bed. I turned off the lights and blocked out the light from the windows in my room. I lay down in complete darkness. But what I had done was actually the opposite of what God had just done in the shower.

I allowed darkness to take over that room. (I need you all to catch what I just said). That darkness was just more than turning off the lights. It shifted the atmosphere and took away what God intended to happen in that very moment of desperation. It took me back to a place before He let me up. So now I'm back to crying, and back to saying, "Release me from this pain, make it stop, release me from the pain in my heart." I said that a few more times. He responded, "You want to be released from the hurt and pain but secretly in your heart you want the same pain inflicted on that person. Vengeance is mine," says the Lord. I could do nothing but ask for forgiveness because God was right, I wanted him to feel the same pain I was feeling and worse. So I had to forgive him (which was very hard to do) and then ask God to forgive me. It wasn't until then that I felt the weight of the pain leave me. It didn't happen all at once, but that night it was enough for me to rest, and I slept all night for the first time in months (because it was months I was living like that).

I delayed my own deliverance because I couldn't let go because I couldn't accept what had happened, because I had unforgiveness in my heart, because I was pretending that I wa

OK in public but dying in private. I just had to keep saying, Lord, just help me to be OK with the dissolution of things. Help me to be OK with disappointment, when people change up on me, or even when I can't have my way. We've got to be careful of the things we ask God to take away, to heal, or to deliver us from when we want to inflict the same hurt onto the ones whom we believe offended us in the first place. Think about it, how can we want grace and mercy for ourselves and want the same withheld from the other person who caused us pain? Those people, like it or not, are still God's children and He loves them just as much as He loves you. But for some of us, it's easier to hold on because we're not done yet, we are unforgiving, we still want revenge, we like the attention it gives us to play the victim's role, and we want closure. Now let's be careful with the word "closure." Let's face it, most times we don't want to let go or move forward because we've convinced ourselves that we need closure first. We need to know why. I'm guilty of that. I always needed to know why. When in reality, what we call closure is just a means to hold onto what we already know we need to let go of. I did this. It felt like losing. It was an excuse to stay right where I was. But that no longer worked for me.

I needed to get out of this wilderness, and I needed out fast. I realized that it was bigger than me, and at this point, I was at the end of my rope. I was finally willing to give up what I'd been holding onto to get what I really needed. So I took God at His word and let Him lead me. I followed Him out of the wilderness. I could see again. I could feel again. I could breathe again. I wasn't weighed down. There was life still left in me. What I learned that day was sometimes we are where God needs us to be. Sometimes we have to go through hell and fire to be molded into something greater. Psalm 42:11 (NLT) says, "Why am I discouraged? Why is my heart so sad? I will put my hope in God! I will praise Him again — my Savior and my God!" In the commentary of the book, I found this interesting. It read:

"Depression is one of the most common emotional ailments. One antidote for depression is to meditate on the record of God's goodness to His people. This will take your mind off the present situation and give hope that it will improve. It will focus your thoughts on God's ability to help you rather than on your inability to help yourself. When you feel depressed take advantage of this Psalm's antidepressant, read the bible's account of God's goodness and meditate on them." (Zondervan)

Now, that help may not come right away (as you see it took me years), but in the waiting, praise Him. I believe if I had done this earlier on in life I wouldn't have wasted so much time trying to go on in my own strength. Our praise binds the hands of the enemy, and it confuses them. It reminds me that His grace and mercy are unlike anything, and it was not just for others, but it was for me also. It's for you, reader, also. His word was fact true. He loves us all the same, whether we believe it or not. Whether we think we're deserving or not. He does not need our permission to do anything, especially to love us. He can't not love us, because that is who He is. I found that it's a little easier on me to be on His side, in His will, rather than fighting against it. I declared that all the hell I went through produced enough faith to move God's hand. Let the healing begin.

HEALING & RESTORATION
(TAKE BACK YOUR LIFE)

It took me 20 years to finally get here. And some days I still struggle — as we all do. But this process was necessary. Your process is necessary.

Healing requires a high level of commitment to yourself. Are you ready?

Let's start with this question: what's the first thing you must do to start the healing process? As Dr. Elisa LaShell Harney would say, "You can't fix what you won't face." I believe that to be very true. The first thing you must do to heal is to be willing to accept the truth (good or bad) before you can move on from the lie that has been holding you hostage.

I want you to take a moment and think about what I just said. Now, what lie is holding you hostage? Are you thinking about it? Good. Now, acknowledge it, sit in it. Do you feel the sting of it? Yeah, it hurts, doesn't it? I know. But it's the only way. Come on, let's do this together.

Healing begins the moment you stop pretending it isn't

hurting you. The truth of the matter is, it's really our choice to hold onto it or to release it, as I mentioned in the previous chapter. So the real question is, will you release it? In order for you to get healed, you've got to come clean with yourself. I can't stress that enough. Come clean with yourself. You have to be able to see in the dark until the light consumes you again. What I mean by "see in the dark" is: you simply have to acknowledge what's really there. What's in your mind, in your heart, and what's been anchoring your soul. As we know everything starts with the mind. The mind is meant to absorb information that transforms it into knowledge that then leads it into action. Romans 12:2 (KJV) says: "And be not conformed to this world: but be ye transformed by the renewing of your mind, that ye may prove what is that good, and acceptable, and perfect, will of God." Sometimes we have too much going on in our mind that it seems as if everything is running together. We lose focus and are unable to make sound decisions. We also lose touch with reality and who we really are. We cannot see what is before us in its true form. When this happens, all we can do is ask God to give us understanding and to remove the scales from our eyes so we can see. Isaiah 59:10 (KJV) says, "We grope for the wall like the blind, and we grope as if we had no eyes: we stumble at noon day as in the night; we are in desolate places as dead men." Imagine that it's daytime and we see as if it's midnight all the time. If we can't see no better than dead men, we can't see at all. Our eyes work but we're spiritually blind.

So what do we do? We make stuff up. We see what we want to see and we take it as truth. But this type of dysfunction is dangerous and will distort your reality and your discernment. Now some of the things we're struggling within our minds as it relates to us were not all caused by an outside force or person. Let's tell the truth. Some things, if not most, were caused by us. It is because of our very own words, and now we're watching it manifest. Let me ask you this, when was the last time you put your mouth on yourself in a positive way? It was years and years before I got this for myself. Don't let this be you. Plant new word seeds about yourself, like positive words of affirmation. Lift yourself up daily as you would do for others. When I did this, it changed the way I saw everything. But before you can get to this point, you're going to have to figure some things out first.

So let's talk about it: Who are you? Not your name, position, title, or the most common response "I'm a child of God." Let's dig deeper than that. Who are you? When I was asked this question, my response was always the same. I am Nicole and am a mother. Outside of that, I had nothing else really to say. But after I got God involved, my answer changed. It can happen for you as well, you just have to talk with Him, read His word, and, most of all, believe what He says. Now, this won't happen overnight. It is a process that will cause you to unlearn what you always thought was true about yourself. So once we figure that out, we can move on to how we handle the things in our lives. When we encounter an issue or some type of conflict, our natural response is to become defensive. It's a way to protect ourselves. For me, I ignored it until it blew up. And it came out however it came out and whoever got it just got it, underserved or not. Yes, I was a mess. But the good news is, I no longer handle life that way. I take things one day at a time. I could tell I was changing by the way I handled the very people who mishandled me. I don't always agree with what may be happening or the outcome of it, but I have come to understand that everything that happens is teaching me something else. It's preparing me for something bigger than what's happening at that moment. The old cliché "Everything happens for a reason" is in fact true. Just keep living and you'll see. There is purpose in it all.

Once we figure these things out, we can then live in our truth. We need to stop pretending everything is OK when it isn't. It's OK to not be OK. We become toxic to ourselves and kill ourselves slowly when we don't stop pretending. This is why it hurts so much and for so long. We get sick physically, mentally, and spiritually. They're all connected. And let me tell you, mental illness is a whole beast on its own. You can't sleep, you can't eat, you can't focus, you can't function, and you become irritable in some if not all ways. Everything will bother you. But there is hope. For me, I had reached the end of my rope and finally sought counseling. It was the best decision I could have ever made. Most of us grew up hearing, "Therapy is for crazy people." That stigma is why so many of us are in the messes we're in now. Therapy was something I never thought I would need. But life at that point gave me no other option. I had reached a dark place in my life and had no choice but to seek help. I met with Dr. Tracy Knighton of NOVA Counseling & Consulting Services and explained what I needed. Let me tell you, those conversations revealed a lot. Yes, it was uncomfortable, sometimes embarrassing, and shameful, but it was necessary. I remember one homework assignment she gave me where I was instructed to write a letter from my current age to my younger self (at the age where I became lost) and a letter from my younger self to my older self. It was meant to bring some type of clarity as to what happened between those years. The writing part was easy, it just poured out. But reading it back to myself out loud was difficult. As I said before, it hits differently when you hear it audibly. Try it sometime, it answered a lot of questions for me. I didn't let that one assignment deter me, though. I continued through the process. I did the work, I was transparent, open, and I wanted to get better. It held me accountable, and it was a lifesaver. If nothing else, INVEST in your mental health. Just think how much further along I would have been if I just got the help I really needed sooner. Imagine what it could do for you. It's never too late. Only you will know when you're ready to take that step. Just don't wait 20-plus years. Some things are meant to happen but are not meant to last forever, and the more you accept what is, the less you'll be controlled by what was. Never get so comfortable in your mess that you forget that your happiness still matters. You matter!

Outside of therapy, to get to where you need to be, remember He got you.

Ask God to reveal who He is.

Ask God to reveal who He called you to be.

Ask God to reveal what He called you to do.

Ask God for instructions on how to get there or how to do it.

Make this journey personal. Not only for your benefit but for the people who are depending on you to get yourself together. Stop fighting against yourself and stop robbing God of His glory. Now get up, shake yourself off and take back your life. If I can do it, I know without a doubt you can too. We got this

DANCE SAVED ME

This is my favorite chapter of the book. For so many years I sat on the third row at my church, Sunday after Sunday, and left the same way I came. Yes, you heard that correctly, I left the same way I came. At that time, I figured just attending was enough, or it should have been enough. I figured if I went enough it was God's job then to fix everything. Isn't that like most of us? We want to just show up and expect God to give us a microwave answer to all our problems. "Fix it, God," is what I would say often, but no answer. I engaged in the services, and I listened to the word being preached, but that didn't get His attention either. I would even find myself going up regularly to the altar Sunday after Sunday, hoping that would be the day, but it wasn't.

At the end of the day, on a drive back home, something was still missing. I had a hole in my soul that I could not fill. Now I'm getting angry because it seems as if God isn't listening to me. Does that sound familiar to you? We get mad with God because we can't have our way. We get mad because God won't come right then and there and give us what we want. Yeah, I know, it's crazy, but we do act that way. No matter what I did or got involved in, nothing changed.

Things started to get worse. I was catching hell from every angle and the enemy wasn't letting up. He was having a field day with my life. Now one Sunday after regular service, the Dance Ministry ministered in dance. It was my first time seeing it in person. I had heard of it but didn't quite know what it was. I thought it was just dancing, but boy was I wrong. It was so much more than that. So now every time they danced, I found myself up out of my seat and flowing with them as if I had rehearsed. I would say to myself, "Girl, what are you doing, sit down." But I couldn't. As long as they were up, I was up.

A few years had passed and one Sunday the dance ministry leader, Mrs. Carolyn Price (who I now call My Moses), stopped me and said, "I'm waiting for you." I responded, "Waiting on me?" with a puzzled look on my face. She responded, "Yes, for you to join the dance ministry." I immediately said, "Oh no, Ma'am, that's not for me." "I'll wait," she said as she walked away. Well, that short conversation ignited something in me that I didn't know was there. It was a fire that needed fuel. But I denied it and watered it down because I thought I wasn't good enough or worthy enough to dance before God's people. Especially in front of people who knew me from way back when. You see how we can block our own blessings? How we can delay the things God has set in motion? I immediately dismissed what she said because my past shame had me bound. But even still, my spirit would not let up. Every time I saw them dance since then, that fire grew hotter and hotter. It was calling me, but I was too afraid. I tried to fight it, but I couldn't fight it anymore.

That next Sunday, I asked Mrs. Price to join the dance ministry, and my life has never been the same since. She accepted me as I was and opened her heart to me in a way I was never used to. She allowed me to be who I was and opened the door for me to grow. It wasn't easy because I was still wrestling with not feeling good enough. She poured into me so much that I could never repay her. It was very easy for me to follow her as a leader because everything she did, she did in love. There's a humbleness about her. She's quiet but she's one of God's secret weapons. Imagine having a leader like that. One who is after God's own heart. That's who I had in my corner. Even in her correction, she would do in love. She held me accountable and never stopped encouraging me. And because of who she is, I started becoming more comfortable and excited about where I was being led.

Now here's where the story gets interesting. One night during rehearsal, a song was playing in the background and as I walked in, I began to dance. I didn't even realize what I was doing. She looked at me like God had just revealed something to her. She said, "That's your song you'll minister to." I was like, "Say what now?" In my mind, I'm thinking, "Now this woman has got to be crazy. I just recently joined, I didn't know much, and now she wants me to do a solo." But that was all she said, "That's your song." As usual, I brushed it off and went on about my way.

I decided to play the song and listen to it as I drove home. Let me tell you, I was in everybody's lane because I could not be still. I was stirred up and couldn't quite understand it. This has never happened before. What was going on? I went home, showered, and got in bed. I was tired but could not sleep. I w still stirred up. If you've ever been stirred up, you understand what I'm talking about. So, I started listening to the song again as I lay in bed. I found myself doing the same thing as in the car. I could not be still. Next thing I knew, my spirit said get up and dance. I lay there for a minute, like what is happening. But my spirit kept nudging me to get up and dance. Finally, I obeyed and got up. Not only did I get up — I got up and put on my full garment. The only garment I had.

I moved my living room table and chairs back and just started dancing. Before you know it, I had danced to the whole song and created a whole new dance. I kept asking myself, "What was happening?" So, I danced it again, and this time I recorded it. I sent the video to Moses. Her response was, "You will minister on Sunday." Say what now? That gave me one day to get this dance together. I was terrified and very hesitant. But the more I thought about not doing it, the calmer I became. It all just didn't make sense to me.

Well, Sunday had arrived, and it was the end of a regular service. Moses went up to the front of the church, talked to the congregation, and introduced me. I felt a heaviness as I walked to the front while she was still talking. It was like a weight was trying to hold me back, but I made it to the front anyway. I believe the heaviness I was feeling was God's last reminder that everything that was weighing me down...was about to be released. He needed me to be in the right posture.

He needed me to surrender. He needed me to bring it all to the surface and lay it at His feet, so when it was all said and done, I'd know that it was nobody but Him that released me. The music was set to go, I took my position and the sound man hit play. I took a deep breath. I didn't see anyone and I didn't hear anyone. All I know is the Holy Spirit danced with me that day. It was like it was just me and Him. He took over and He had His way. The heaviness that was on me fell off. The chains were loose, the strongholds were broken, I could see, I could feel, I could breathe, and I felt His love and His hands on me. My faith moved God's hand that day, and I was set free.

Those of us who dance and have been freed in our dance will understand what I just said. It's a feeling like no other. I will never forget that day. It was a healing experience. I ministered to the song "Better" by Jessica Reedy. I wore a green and white garment to represent healing, prosperity, new life, growth, hope, and peace. If you get a chance, listen to the song, listen to the words of the song. Think back on what you've read already and you will understand why it means so much to me even to this day. Imagine if I had never listened to Moses. Imagine if she wasn't connected to the Spirit to first say anything to me at all. I probably would still be sitting on that third row in church. I would still be bound, and I wouldn't have written this book. I am forever grateful for what Moses did for me. I could nev repay her, but I'm thankful she obeyed God. She is my sister, my friend, and we have a covenant bond for life. She's family, and I love her dearly. I wish I could attach that dance to this book so you can see what God does for His people when we allow Him to have His way. I had a head-on collision with His glory, and it fell like fresh wind and it burned like new fire. I believe it happened the way it happened because I was desperate and needed something different. There was a cry in my spirit that only He could comfort and restore. I'm getting too excited just thinking about it.

Believe me when I tell you, it does get better, if only you believe. On February 18, 2018, dance saved my life. A few months later, I enrolled in GOLD Praise Dance School of Ministry (GOLD stands for God's Ordained Liturgical Dance). I took a six-month dance class under the leadership and guidance of Apostle Pamela Grimes. This class is not designed to teach you how to dance, but it frees you so you can dance. While in this class, my thought process changed, I could apply dance biblically, I saw myself differently, and I was able to break free from things that were still hidden. We would meet every week and there was always a new revelation. The whole program exceeded my expectations and gave me a better understanding of dance. Not only was I learning about dance itself, but I was also learning why I dance and the power behind it. This process pushed me to a higher level in my relationship with God and it was a life-changing journey. I studied, I prayed, I was open, I allowed myself to be vulnerable, I was transparent, and, most of all, I made the necessary sacrifices. This process wasn't easy, yet it was because I was in a safe place.

Thank you, Apostle, for allowing me to be a part of your school. Thank you for stretching me and taking me out of my comfort zone week after week. Your dedication to your school does not go unnoticed. Blessings to you and continued success with your school. When I tell you my life has never been the same, I mean just that. I thank God He put a comma where man had put a period. On April 6, 2019, I was ordained as a Minister of Dance.

GLORY CARRIER!!!

MADE WHOLE

I often hear a lot of people say, "I want to be made whole." But do we really know what it means? The definition of "whole" can be defined in many ways. It is all of; a thing that is complete in itself. Those are good ways to define "whole." But my favorite definition is: in an unbroken or undamaged state; in one piece. Just that definition, "in itself," is enough to paint a clear picture. Unfortunately, some of us are not whole. We walk around broken. And we're so broken that we can't even work together as one body within ourselves. "Broken" is defined as having been fractured or damaged and no longer in one piece or in working order. When we find ourselves in this state, nine times out of 10 it's in several different areas of our lives. It's never just one thing because they are all connected. For me, it was my mind. It was all over the place. And because everything starts in the mind, it affected everything else. I was making bad decisions, I was indecisive, I was unfocused, and

I was unbalanced. Nothing I did seemed to get things back in order, it would just get more chaotic. Everything was out of order. I was operating in dysfunction as if it was normal.

This state of living had become my way of life for years. But (don't you just love when God interrupts your life with a BUT) it wasn't until after I was introduced to dance that I knew what I was missing, and I wanted it. I wanted to be made whole. But only God could do that. All I had to do was ask. Was it really that simple? In my carnal thinking, it could not be. There was no way it was that easy. Then I remembered the story of the man paralyzed in the Bible in John 5. He was by the healing pool for 38 years waiting on someone to put him in the pool. Jesus asked him directly in John 5:6 (KJV), "Wilt thou be made whole?" Instead of a direct answer, the man gave Jesus an excuse that no one would help him get in the pool when the water was troubled or that someone gets in before he can. Who does that sound like? Sounds like us, doesn't it? On one hand we want this and that, but on the other, we're full of excuse about the same thing. Jesus doesn't want to hear our excuses nor does He care for them. All He wants to know is if you want to be made whole. But this only works if you believe that you can be made whole and that Jesus can do it.

See, we can say anything, but the question is, do you believe what you're asking for? Do you have faith in what you're asking for? Well, I finally got it. I understood what I was really asking me. And my answer was yes. Yes, Lord, I want to be made whole. After you say yes, just let Him do the work. He said, "You are made whole. I did it this way because I needed you to come from a place of authenticity when you reach My people. Now go do the work I called you to do." He had need of me, and I just needed to be made whole first. There was an assignment waiting for me. I had work to do. Now that I'm whole, I can effectively minister to people in the same conditions I won over. Now I get the meaning behind the question, "wilt thou be made whole?" Do you get it? I hope so because it's necessary. If you don't let your past die, it won't let you live.

Be Made Whole!!

IT WAS NECESSARY

Iused to hate when people would say, "Everything happens for a reason."

It would anger me to hear because to me it meant that I deserved it. Like I got exactly what I asked for. But that's untrue.

Now that I know better, I do believe everything happens for a reason. As I think back on all the things I've done, said, have been through, and had to deal with, it made me who I am today. The heartbreak, the breakdowns, the resentment, the abandonment, the rejections, the failures, living paycheck to paycheck, the loneliness, the isolation, the pain, the destruction, the self-made prison, the self-torture, the shame, the guilt, the financial hardships, and everything else were indeed worth it. My pain actually had a purpose. It was necessary. Had I not been through what I've been through, I don't think I would be here. And if I was still here, I wouldn't be the person I am today. It's all a part of His divine plan.

As He says in His word in Jeremiah 29:11 (NIV), "For I know the plans I have for you,' declares the Lord, 'plans to prosper you and not to harm you, plans to give you hope and a future."

Now, this does not mean we won't face hardships; it means that He will see us through them to fulfill His purpose. His will will be done.

God was molding me and preparing me for greater. As I said before, He put me through some things and allowed some things to happen, so that I could come from a place of authenticity when I go before His people. I didn't understand it then, and surely didn't like it, but now I get it. He's very strategic in what He does. We just have to believe in and trust the process. So now, I'm thankful. I no longer fight against Him or His plan, I just humbly ask that He gives me the strength to get through life and for the wisdom to understand His plan. I want what He wants for me. I want to be aligned with His will. I want to leave this place empty and hear the words, "Well done, my good and faithful servant." I want Him to be pleased with everything I do in His name. Now don't get me wrong, it's hard to believe that it's necessary when you're going through it, but He will work it out for your good and that's enough to give Him praise. And now that I believe in His plan, I can boldly walk in my assignments under His power and authority, and so can you.

So don't dismiss what you go through. Don't complain or despise it. Embrace it. It will change your life and bring forth just who He created you to be. It was and is NECESSARY!!!!

THE WEIGHT OF A SILENT VESSEL'S HEART

I wrote this free verse poetry as it was given to me in the Spirit on April 12, 2020, at 4 a.m. It was actually a silent conversation between me and God. Believe me when I tell you, He hears our tears in our silence. It's something about that midnight, early morning hours. Every day I am awakened around the same time. If this happens to you, don't just go back to sleep. That's your time when God wants to commune with you. There are little to no distractions and you can hear clearly. This is what my heart was feeling at the time, and this is how it came out in a conversation with the Spirit:

Day in and day out, I've learned to adjust the temperature of my beating heart. Up and down, down, and up, to match the day as not to give up. There's a hole invisible to the natural eye, where rejection and abandonment lie. They've taken up residence and recruited some friends to make it easier for me to bend. It bends and it pulls, it breaks, and it folds into bigger-sized holes. I've patched it with this and patched it with that, only to discover that it has now gone flat. It's no longer sitting in its place; it's now lying flat on its own pool of hate. I'll pick it up and dust it off quick before the world can see it on my face.

You've become good at covering, just carrying on as if nothing has happened. Bleeding out has become the new normal. You're strong, they say, 'cause you're always there to lift their weight without complaints.

I give and I give, and sometimes run dry. Now I'm left alone, needing to be revived. In my waiting, who will come for me, who will hold my hand, who will it be?

As I look up, the room is empty and filled with the echoes of my own desperate pleas. The outside doesn't see because they really don't know me. This is of my own doing. They go by the covering I've displayed for them to see. A display of always being fine and nothing is ever wrong. Problem is, that's now what I see. I know why I'm here and what I'm to do, but the fight with my reflection is dreary and blue.

Why'd you pick me, I really want to know. Why'd you pick me to uplift your people from places I barely escaped from myself? Why'd you choose me to carry this weight? You said You know what You're doing, and I need not ponder. "For I know the plans I have for you, plans to prosper you and not to harm you." "You asked to be used and this is My way, just trust Me and do what I say."

Obedience is better than sacrifice, but like Paul I cry out to you

Lord, take this thorn away.

Your response was simple, "My grace is sufficient."

But I'm tired, drained, and can't go on.

Your response was simple, "My power is made perfect in weakness. Again, daughter, you asked to be used. You're built for this, and you will not lose. The weight seems heavy because the anointing is great. There's a cost of the oil to flow. My grace will keep you and My love will repair the patches in your heart."

OK, God, let Your will be done. I hear the beating of my heart. It is like an instrument, it's like a drum. That is how I move. That is how I feel. That is who You created me to be. I see the reflection is changing and is no longer blurred. I feel You carrying the load with me. My shoulders are free. I feel You preparing me for new battles I cannot see. A fixed fight, You say. Oh, I like the sound of that. No, this is not a burden, but a privilege. It will strengthen your character. It will build humility.

So come now and purify this heart. Consume me with Your fire until the weight of a silent vessel's heart speaks!!!!

If you've ever been in the trenches, you'd understand these words. It's in His word. Commune with your Father. He will respond in His own unique way. And if you don't know what to say, the Holy Spirit has your back. The word says in Romans 8:26-27 (KJV), "Likewise the Spirit also helpeth our infirmities: for we know not what we should pray for as we ought: but the Spirit itself maketh intercession for us with groanings which cannot be uttered. And He that searcheth the hearts knoweth what is the mind of the Spirit, because He maketh intercession for the saints according to the will of God."

SCRIPTURES TO HELP YOU THROUGH

Below is a list of Scriptures that helped me and carried me through:

Peace

"You will keep in perfect peace those whose minds are steadfast, because they trust in You." Isaiah 26:3 (NIV)

Beauty for Ashes

"and provide for those who grieve in Zion — to bestow on hem a crown of beauty instead of ashes, the oil of joy instead of mourning, and a garment of praise instead of a spirit of despair. They will be called oaks of righteousness, a planting of the Lord for the display of His splendor." Isaiah 61:3 (NIV)

His Forgiveness

"If we confess our sins, He is faithful and just and will forgive us our sins and purify us from all unrighteousness." 1 John 1:9 (NIV)

He Cares

"Cast your cares on the Lord and He will sustain you; He will never let the righteous be shaken." Psalm 55:22 (NIV)

Give Yourself to Him

"Take delight in the Lord, and He will give you the desires of your heart." Psalm 37:4 (NIV)

He's Enough

"But He said to me, 'My grace is sufficient for you, for my power is made perfect in weakness.'" 2 Corinthians 12:9 (NIV)

Be Bold

"For the Spirit God gave us does not make us timid, but gives us power, love and self-discipline." 2 Timothy 1:7 (NIV)

He's Always There (My favorite Scripture)

"For I am the Lord your God who takes hold of your right hand and says to you, Do not fear; I will help you." Isaiah 41:13 (NIV)

He Intercedes for Us

"In the same way, the Spirit helps us in our weakness. We c

not know what we ought to pray for, but the Spirit Himself intercedes for us through wordless groans." Romans 8:26 (NIV)

Keep these Scriptures in mind and/or find Scriptures that speak to you. Study them. Keep them in your heart and it will help you through this necessary journey. Trust the process and believe in His word. My prayer for you is that you would be so covered in His blood that the enemy has to ask permission to touch you. I pray that the ones who are lost would know that He will find you. I pray that the ones who think they're forgotten are reminded that He knows your name. May each one of you find peace, wholeness, and revelation upon reading this book. I pray that you seek His face and His guidance in everything that you do. Believe in yourself. You are worthy and you are loved. You can do it. We got this and we're in this together.

My mantra is #LoveAlone, so let's get to it.

PRAYER OF SALVATION

This book is filled with many life lessons and applicable principles that can immediately be inserted into your life. However, if you desire to reach your full potential in every facet of life, you must know that you can't do it alone.

Oftentimes, we're more focused on our unpredictable horizontal relationships than the unchanging vertical one that matters most. God is our Source, and the only way we can stay plugged in to Him, is through Jesus Christ. If you've never confessed Jesus as your Lord and Savior, there's no better day to do so than today!

To begin a relationship with God through Jesus, all you have to do is confess with your mouth and believe in your heart that Jesus died AND rose for your sins (Romans 10:9-10). If you're tired of trying to fight through life, and you're ready to live life more abundantly, the below prayer is for you.

PRAYER OF SALVATION:

"God in Heaven, I come to You in the name of Jesus Christ. You said in the Bible that if I confess with my mouth that Jesus is my Lord and believe in my heart that You have raised Him from the dead, I will be saved. So right now, I am confessing that I believe Jesus died on the cross and rose 3 days later so that I may live. I accept Him now and am confessing that He is My Lord and Savior. Heavenly Father, I also repent and ask for forgiveness for any and all sins that I have committed against you, in Jesus Name.

God, thank You that when Jesus went to Heaven, You sent Holy Spirit to this earth to be my Helper, Comforter, and Friend, so that I don't have to walk through this life alone. Holy Spirit, I welcome You into my heart right now. Fill me until I overflow. I believe I have received my heavenly language and I WILL speak in my heavenly language (tongues), when I open my mouth to speak, in the mighty name of JESUS CHRIST, amen!"

BEAUTY FOR ASHES: YOUR STORY

Now it's your turn to tell your story! Use these next few pages to write your testimony about how God has given you beauty for ashes. I want you to really take a second to think about the questions before you answer them. Be completely honest and transparent with yourself in this moment. Write it down exactly how you feel it in YOUR spirit. Don't second guess yourself, or change your answers to try and make it sound good. Write it down as it is – raw, real, and 100% TRUTH. Are you ready? Let's go!

Who are you?

_____

_____

_____

_____

_____

_____

_____

_____

_____

_____

_____

_____

_____

_____

_____

_____

_____

_____

_____

_____

What do you believe about yourself?

What is God saying about you?

_____

_____

_____

_____

_____

_____

_____

_____

_____

_____

_____

_____

_____

_____

_____

_____

_____

_____

_____

_____

_____

_____

What is God saying to you?

_____

_____

_____

_____

_____

_____

_____

_____

_____

_____

_____

_____

_____

_____

_____

_____

_____

_____

_____

_____

_____

_____

What is God calling you to do?

_____

_____

_____

_____

_____

_____

_____

_____

_____

_____

_____

_____

_____

_____

_____

_____

_____

_____

_____

_____

_____

What are some of your lessons learned?

What revelations have you received along life's journey?

HOMEWORK
Mirror Check Time

Now that you've answered the questions, here comes the hard part. I want you to find a mirror, the biggest mirror in your house, with lots of light, and look at yourself. Answer the questions again. This time, say it out loud. What do you see? What do you hear? Is what you're seeing and hearing, lining up with the questions you just answered? Were your answers true? If what you see or wrote about yourself is contrary to Gods word, that's where you need to start. Your true reflection and identity is in His word. You just must read it and believe it.

#NoMoreAshes

It's time to move forward...FREE!

What's your plan of action to enjoy the BEAUTY that you've received?

_____

_____

_____

_____

_____

_____

_____

_____

_____

_____

_____

_____

_____

_____

_____

_____

_____

_____

_____

ABOUT THE AUTHOR

Nicole E. Holmes is a native of St Croix U.S. Virgin Islands where she resided for 17 years. She made her way to Albany, GA, in 1993 to attend Albany State University, where she graduated with a bachelor's in criminal justice. She pursued her career in law enforcement and served her community as a police officer for 10 years. She has now moved on to a different career path in the Supply Chain and Logistics Management field. She now works as a supply technician. She is a member of the St. James Missionary Baptist Church in Baconton, Ga. She is a mother of two children, daughter, Destiney, and son, Kevin, Jr. She was called to dance in 2018 where she is currently a part of the Grateful Praise Dance Ministry. She was ordained as a Minister of Dance in 2019 from God's Ordained Liturgical Dance (GOLD, Inc). She is now a published author and still has a lot more to say. She is dedicated to uplifting people and encouraging them by sharing her testimony. Her transparency allows her to reach those in the trenches. Under the authority of God and the continued support from her church leaders, family, and friends, she is dedicated to reaching as many as she can through her ministry in dance and the word of her testimony. She can do all this because God gave her **Beauty for Ashes!!**

15102532R00049